STRINGS IN STEP

violin book 1 WITH AUDIO

JAN DOBBINS

MUSIC DEPARTMENT

OXFORD
UNIVERSITY PRESS

TEACHERS' NOTES

This book introduces pupils to the basics of string playing. Information is presented in a logical order and reinforced at each stage. The series is suitable for group or individual tuition.

Technique, care of the instrument, note reading, sight-reading, intonation, improvisation, and composition are introduced and consolidated through the use of diagrams, games, and worksheets.

Pupils' progress

An average rate of progress for 7–9-year-olds would be the completion of each section in ten to twelve weeks. Although new information is introduced throughout the book the material does not become any more difficult to play after the traditional tunes on pages 41 and 42. This encourages children to move on to the end of the book with a feeling of success and gives time for the establishment of a good technique.

Pupils are encouraged to take an interest in their own progress by keeping a record of weekly practice and by planning their own concert performances. The achievement record, to be filled in by the teacher, indicates progress to parents and children while increasing the pupils' feelings of success and generating enthusiasm to continue.

How to use the book

1. Keep left-hand fingerwork and bowing separate until both are firmly established.
2. Use the bowing patterns often.
3. When introducing new tunes or exercises, ask pupils to listen to, then sing and clap each exercise before they play. The short exercises enable pupils to concentrate on technique and intonation as they play.
4. Revise past work thoroughly.
5. Use the colour coding system.
6. Give time to improvisation and composition using bowing and finger patterns as a starting point.

Colour coding

To help pupils develop their understanding of which finger to use and where to place it, use the colour coding system. Pupils should be encouraged, under supervision if necessary, to colour in all the charts which show finger numbers, letter names, and notes. When teaching in large groups, put dots of the correct colour on each diagram so that they can be coloured in at home.

First finger—red	Third finger—green
Second finger—yellow	Fourth finger—blue

Piano accompaniments P

All tunes and exercises which have piano accompaniments are marked 'P'. Accompaniments are provided for all tunes and exercises in Book 1, with the exception of exercises which cannot be played in ensemble with all instruments, and the rounds.

The Open Strings Pizzicato (Pupil Book pages 10 and 11)

The accompaniments are lyrical and exciting enough for the pupils to feel that they are playing real pieces right from the start. Later, these pieces can be played with the bow.

Pizzicato Tunes on the D String (Pupil Book page 13)

Accompaniments are given for all the tunes in E, A, D, G, and C majors so that pupils can practise using the finger pattern on each string as they become familiar with the tunes. A tune using the second finger is included for cellists only.

The tunes can be played using the bow as pupils become more proficient. Some of the tunes appear further on in the book in notated form, and pupils' familiarity with them encourages note reading.

The fourth finger is introduced on page 13. Violin and viola pupils can be encouraged to play the 'Fourth Finger March' regularly as preparation for the introduction of the fourth finger in Section 3.

Bowing Patterns (Pupil Book page 19)

These can be introduced at the teacher's discretion. It is helpful to use the bowing pattern rhythms when learning each of the major scales. Examples of accompaniments for these are given in the keys of A, D, G, and C majors.

How to use the audio tracks on the Companion Website

All of the exercises and pizzicato pieces are performed once on each track. All of the named pieces from page 28 onwards appear twice on each track. Violin, viola, and cello pupils can play straight through each track as all of the exercises and pieces are compatible for all three instruments unless specified otherwise (e.g. track 12, which is for cello only). Brief introductions (usually the last two bars of the piano accompaniment) have been added to all of the pieces and exercises which have no written introduction in the Piano Book. Each of the rounds on page 51 is preceded by a count-in of one bar. Bowing and note reading exercises which do not have a piano accompaniment are not included on the Companion Website; nor are the scales. Track details are given on pages 63–4 of the Pupil Book.

Ensemble playing

Encourage two-part ensemble playing from the start. Use hand clapping, knee slapping, and finger clicking for accompaniments to the tunes. Half the group play, the other half accompany with percussive rhythms.

Try 'I Hear Thunder' (Pupil Book page 33) as a round when pupils are familiar with the notes. 'Merry Dance' and 'Satellite Serenade' can be played as solos by the individual instruments or as three-part ensembles. 'Little Bird' has an easy second part to accommodate pupils in group lessons who progress at different rates and to provide an opportunity for duet work. The cello book contains a second part for 'Moon Waltz' to introduce cello pupils to the idea of playing the bass line in ensemble. Finally, the rounds are a good way to introduce four-part ensemble playing.

NB Tunes and exercises which cannot be played in ensemble with the other instruments in the series are indicated by an asterisk, ✳ .

Jan Dobbins 2003

CONTENTS

SECTION 3

The Violin

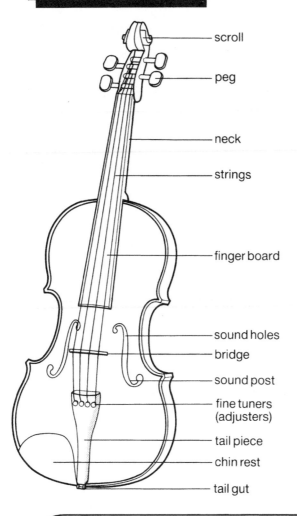

- scroll
- peg
- neck
- strings
- finger board
- sound holes
- bridge
- sound post
- fine tuners (adjusters)
- tail piece
- chin rest
- tail gut

The Bow

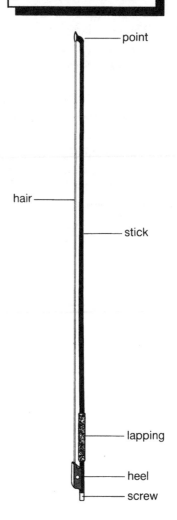

- point
- hair
- stick
- lapping
- heel
- screw

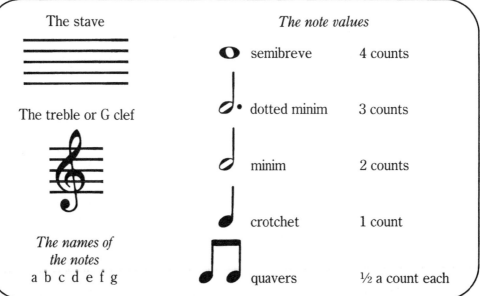

The stave

The treble or G clef

The names of the notes
a b c d e f g

The note values

𝆱	semibreve	4 counts
𝅗𝅥.	dotted minim	3 counts
𝅗𝅥	minim	2 counts
𝅘𝅥	crotchet	1 count
𝅘𝅥𝅮𝅘𝅥𝅮	quavers	½ a count each

Care of the Violin and Bow

1. Always put the violin away in the case after practice, wrapped in a cloth.

2. Never leave the violin in the sun or near a radiator.

3. Tighten the hair before you play.
    Loosen the hair before you put the bow away.

4. Remember to resin your bow.
    Never put anything but resin on your bow.

5. Avoid touching the bow hair with your fingers.

6. Leave a duster in your case to clean your violin and keep it free from resin.

Balancing the violin

The Violin

Name the parts of the violin:

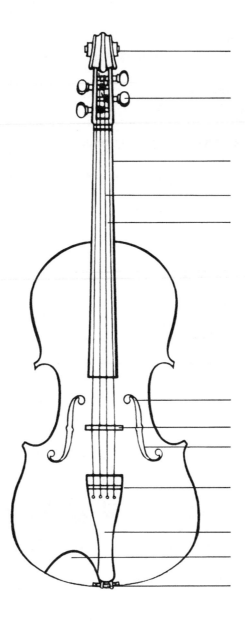

Scroll	Peg
Neck	Fingerboard
Strings	Bridge
Sound hole	Sound post
Fine tuners	Tail piece
Tail gut	Chin rest

The Names of the Violin Strings

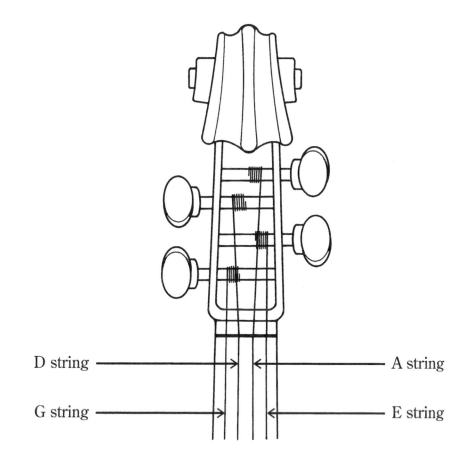

D string ————→ ←———— A string

G string ————→ ←———— E string

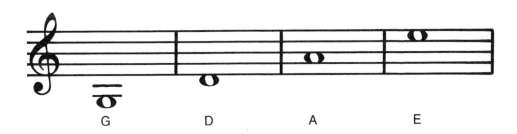

G   D   A   E

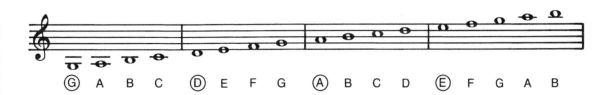

G A B C D E F G A B C D E F G A B

The Open Strings Pizzicato

'Pizzicato' means to pluck the string.

P ### The D string

Count:	1	2	3	4
	D	D	D	D
	D	D	D	D
	D	D	D	D
	D	D	D	D

P ### The A string

Count:	1	2	3	4
	A	A	A	A
	A	A	A	A
	A	A	A	A
	A	A	A	A

P ### The D and A strings

Count:	1	2	3	4
	D	D	D	D
	A	A	A	A
	D	D	D	D
	A	A	D	D

P

Pizzicato in Waltz Time

Count:	1	2	3	1	2	3
	A	A	A	A	A	A
	D	D	D	D	D	D
	A	A	A	A	A	A
	D	–	–	D	–	–

The E string

Count:	1	2	3	4
	E	E	E	E
	E	E	E	E
	E	E	E	E
	E	E	E	E

P

The G string

Count:	1	2	3	4
	G	G	G	G
	G	G	G	G
	G	G	G	G
	G	G	G	G

P

All four strings

Count:	1	2	3	4
	G	G	G	G
	D	D	D	D
	A	A	A	A
	E	E	E	E

P

String Waltz

Count:	1	2	3	1	2	3
	E	E	E	Λ	A	A
	D	D	D	D	D	D
	G	G	G	D	D	D
	A	A	A	D	–	–

The Left Hand Finger Numbers

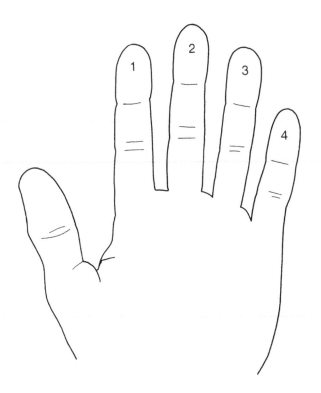

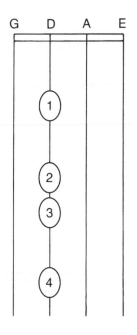

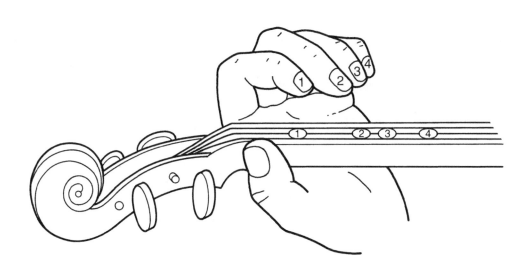

Pizzicato Tunes on the D String

P   *Hopscotch*

```
0  0  0  0     1  1  1  1     0  0  0  0     1  1  1  1
0  0  0  0     1  1  1  1     1  1  1  1     0  –  0  –
```

P   *Hill Climbing*

```
0  0  0  0     1  1  1  1     2  2  2  2     3  3  3  3
2  2  2  2     1  1  1  1     0  0  0  0     0  –  0  –
```

P   *Moonlight*

```
0  0  0  1     2  –  1  –     0  2  1  1     0  –  –  –
0  0  0  1     2  –  1  –     0  2  1  1     0  –  –  –
```

P   *Rainbows*

```
0  0  2  2     1  1  3  –     0  0  2  2     1  1  1  –
2  2  2  2     3  3  3  –     3  3  2  2     1  1  0  –
```

P   *Jumping Jack*

```
0  1  2  0     1  2  3  –     2  2  2  2     1  1  1  –
0  1  2  0     1  2  3  –     2  2  1  1     0  0  0  –
```

P*   *Fourth Finger March*

```
0  1  2  3     4  4  4  4     4  3  2  1     0  –  0  –
```

When you can play these tunes on the D string try them on the A, E or G string.

Concert Performance Idea

Choose a tune you can play really well and think of some words to fit the tune. Then try out this plan:

INTRODUCTION	Count 4 twice;
TUNE ON E	Pizzicato;
LINK	Count 4 twice;
TUNE ON A	Play pizzicato and sing the words;
LINK	Count 4 twice;
TUNE ON D	With the bow, or pizzicato with singing;
LINK	Count 4 twice;
TUNE ON G	Pizzicato.

The Bow

Name the parts of the bow:

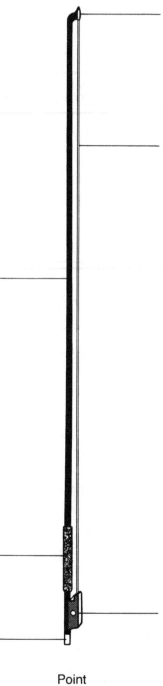

Point
Hair
Heel
Screw
Lapping
Stick

The Bow Hold

Prepare the bow hold by
making a circle with your
thumb and middle finger:

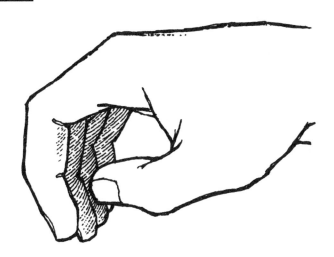

The thumb should be curved
and flexible with the right
corner of the thumbnail
against the stick.

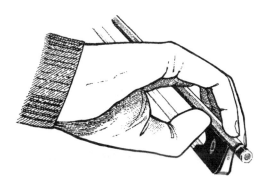

The second and third fingers rest lightly
over the bow stick.

The little finger must stand on the stick and
curve gently.

Imagine that your bow is a bird:
if you hold it too tightly you will kill it;
if you hold it too lightly
it will fly away.

Note Learning Game

Hold your hand out and pretend it is the stave. Your fingers are the lines of the stave. The spaces between your fingers are the spaces of the stave. Use these sentences to help you remember the names of the notes on the lines and in the spaces.

The lines – EVERY GOOD BABY DESERVES FUN

The spaces – DOGS FIGHT AND CATS EAT GOLDFISH

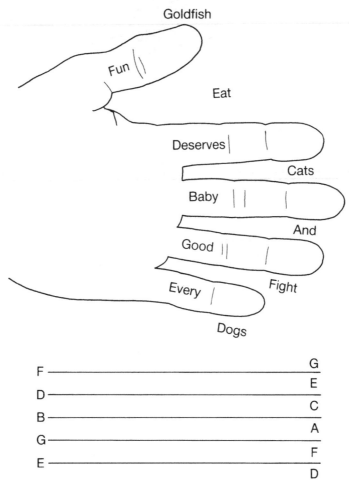

Play this game with a friend: point to a finger or a space and your friend will tell you its letter name.

Leger Lines

Some notes which the violin plays are too high or too low to fit onto the stave. They are written on LEGER LINES.

Bars and Barlines

Music is written on a STAVE:

It is divided into BARS by BARLINES:

Bar   Barline

Time Signatures

The numbers at the beginning of a piece of music are called the TIME SIGNATURE. They tell you how many beats to count in each bar.

$\frac{4}{4}$ count 4 in each bar

$\frac{3}{4}$ count 3 in each bar

$\frac{2}{4}$ count 2 in each bar

You will learn more about time signatures as you work through this book.

Bowing Signs

The Down Bow sign:

To play a 'down' bow, put your bow on the string and move your bowing arm *away* from your body.

The Up Bow sign: V

To play an 'up' bow, put your bow on the string and move your bowing arm *towards* your body.

18

Bowing Patterns

Play them every day.

P

Upper half

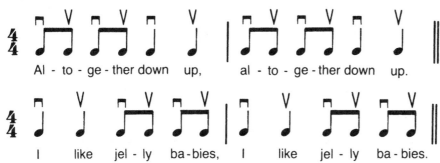

$\frac{4}{4}$ Al - to - ge - ther down up, al - to - ge - ther down up.

$\frac{4}{4}$ I like jel - ly ba - bies, I like jel - ly ba - bies.

Whole bow – upper half – whole bow – lower half

$\frac{4}{4}$ Red roof tops, red roof tops.

Lower half – whole bow – upper half – whole bow

$\frac{4}{4}$ Down up down up, stroke the bow down, up down up down, stroke the bow up.

Whole bows – varied speed

$\frac{3}{4}$ Down bow, up, down bow, up, down bow, up, down.

Repeated down bows

$\frac{4}{4}$ Down, lift, down, lift, down, lift, down, lift, stroke the bow down.

19

Basic Knowledge

1. Draw a ring around the notes which are on a line. Put a cross (X) under the notes which are in a space:

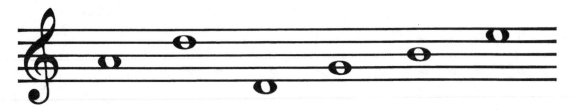

2. This note is D. Copy the note in the places marked:

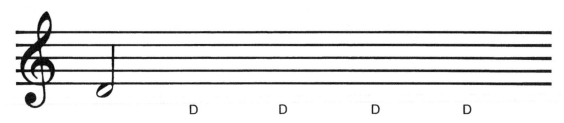

3. This note is E. Copy the note in the places marked:

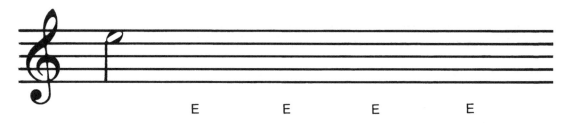

4. This note is B. The stem can go up or down. Copy the note in the places marked and choose which way you would like the stem to go:

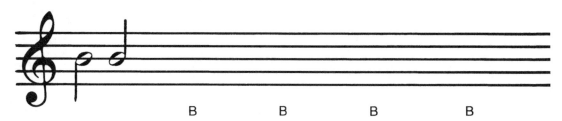

5. Practise drawing the treble clef:

The Open Strings

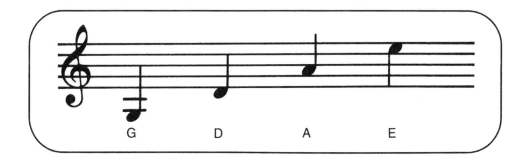

The D string

Count: 1 2 3 4

The A string

Count: 1 2 3 4

The E string

Count: 1 2 3 4

The G string

Count: 1 2 3 4

21

The Crotchet

Each note receives one count.

The Minim

Each note receives two counts.

Count: 1 2 3 4

Minims on Two Strings

Is your right thumb bent?

The Semibreve

Each note receives four counts.

Bowing Exercises on Open Strings

24

The Semibreve Rest

Each rest receives four counts.

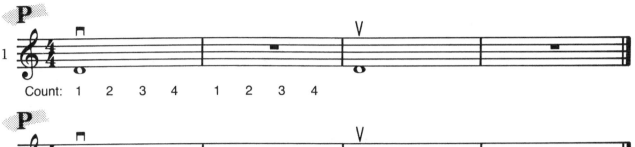

The Minim Rest

Each rest receives two counts.

The Crotchet Rest

Each rest receives one count.

The Rest Tests

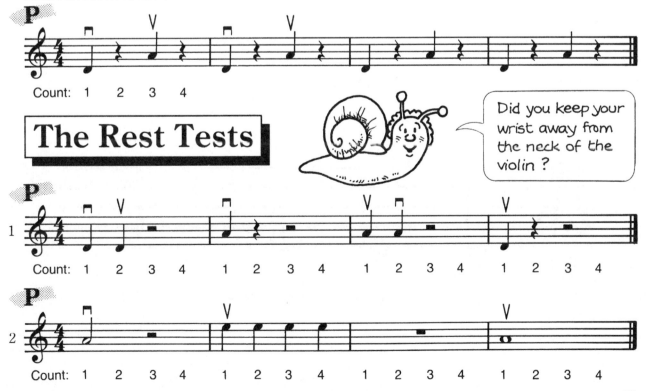

Did you keep your wrist away from the neck of the violin?

The D String Notes

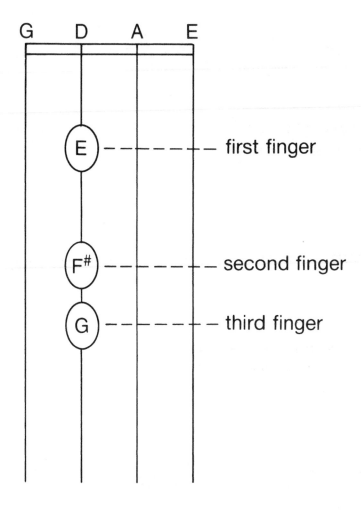

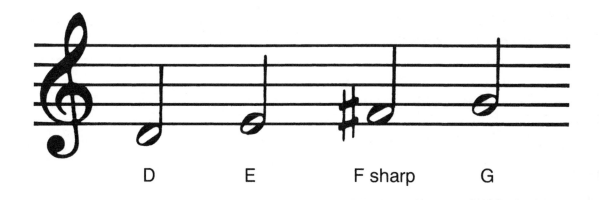

The A String Notes

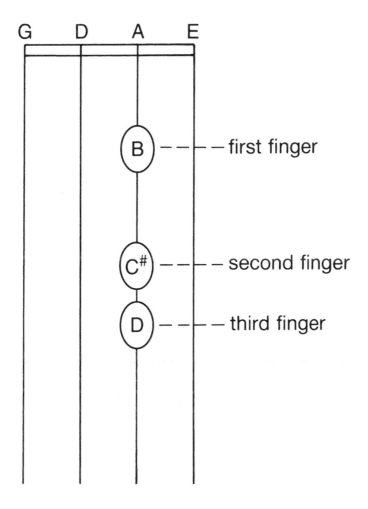

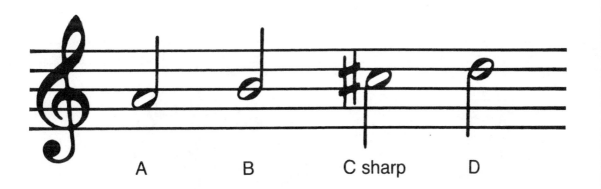

The First Finger on the D String

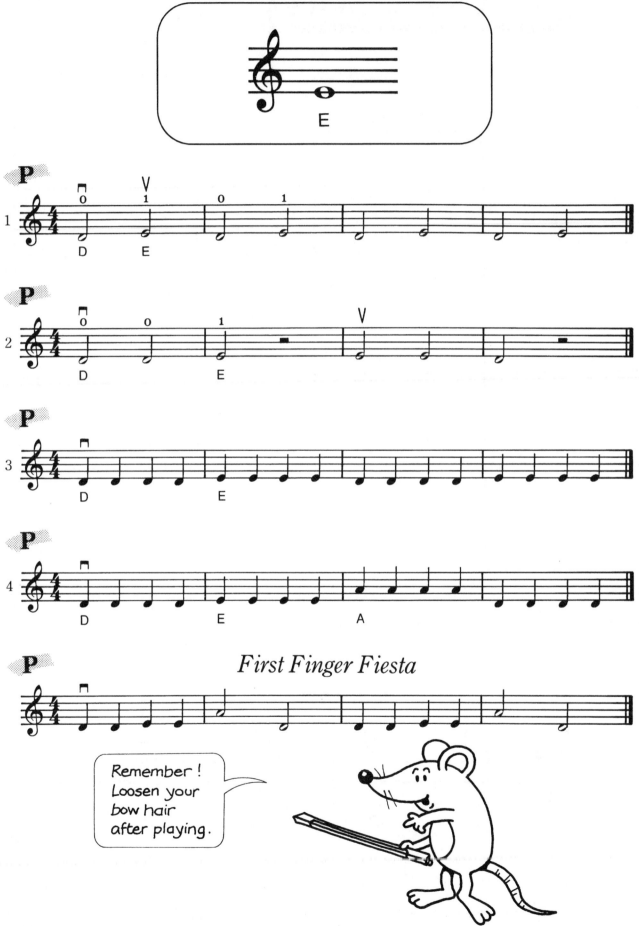

The First Finger on the A String

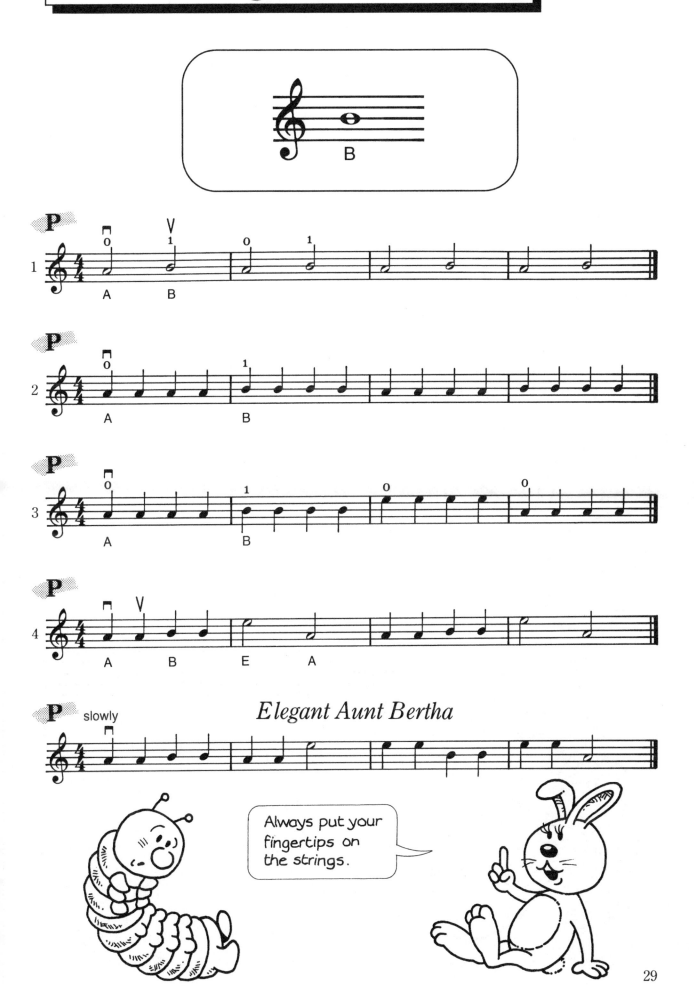

COLOU

R AND PLAY

Carefree Crotchets

G   D   E

A   B   E

Musical Minims

G   D   E   A   B   E

Smooth Semibreves

G   D   E   A   B   E

31

The Second Finger on the D String

F sharp

This is the sharp sign: ♯ It makes the note one semitone higher. It lasts for the whole bar in which it is written.

Going Shopping

Sea Melody

The Second Finger on the A String

The Third Finger on the D String

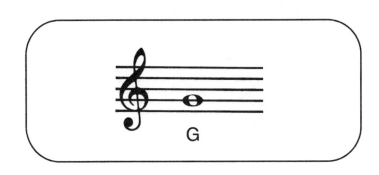

G

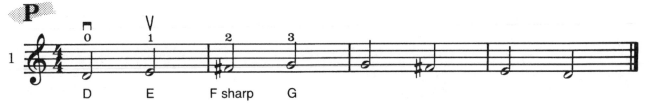

D   E   F sharp   G

D   E   F sharp   G

Level Crossing

smoothly

Hill Climbing

Rainbows

34

The Third Finger on the A String

The Scale of D Major

Third Finger First

Swinging

Jumping Jack

Now you are ready to learn the D major scale and arpeggio on page 59.

Name the Notes (i)

Name these notes:

1.

....

2.

....

3.
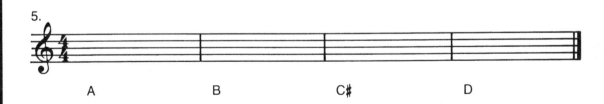

....

Write these notes as semibreves:

4.

D   E   F♯   G

5.

A   B   C♯   D

Quavers

Two quavers make one crotchet beat.

Creeping Jenny

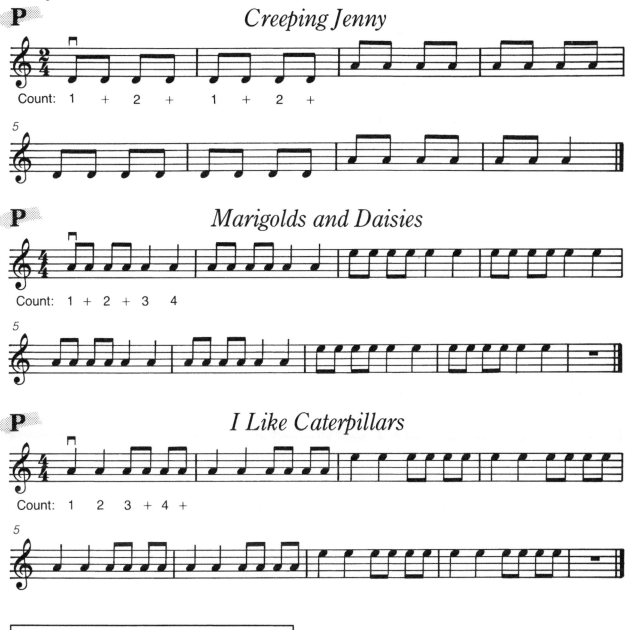

Count: 1 + 2 + 1 + 2 +

Marigolds and Daisies

Count: 1 + 2 + 3 4

I Like Caterpillars

Count: 1 2 3 + 4 +

The Dotted Minim

Each note receives three counts.

Count: 1 2 3

Note Values

1. Write the note value under each note:

2. Now write each bar out as a sum like this:

BAR 1	BAR 2	BAR 3	BAR 4
2			
½			
½			
1			
———	———	———	———
4			
———	———	———	———

3. Write the note value under each note:

4. Now write each bar out as a sum like this:

BAR 1	BAR 2	BAR 3	BAR 4
3			
———	———	———	———
3			
———	———	———	———

5. Write the note value under each note:

6. Now write each bar out as a sum like this:

BAR 1	BAR 2	BAR 3	BAR 4
1			
½			
½			
———	———	———	———
2			
———	———	———	———

The Slur

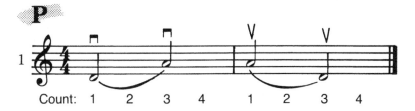

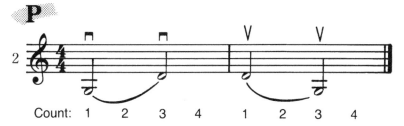

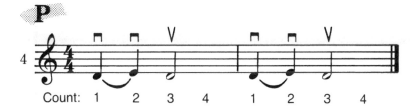

SM-O-O-O-O-TH
B-O-O-O-O-WS

Cross strings smoothly.

Is your bow parallel to the bridge?

39

Key Signatures

The MAJOR KEY which has NO sharps at all is called C MAJOR.

Sharp signs at the beginning of each line of music are called the KEY SIGNATURE and show which KEY the piece of music is in.

This is F sharp. The name of the KEY is G MAJOR. The note G is the KEY NOTE.

F♯ and C♯: the KEY is D MAJOR. The KEY NOTE is D.

F♯, C♯, and G♯: the KEY is A MAJOR. The KEY NOTE is A.

REMEMBER THEM LIKE THIS!

G MAJOR	ONE SHARP	*Fish*
D MAJOR	TWO SHARPS	*Fish* and *Chips*
A MAJOR	THREE SHARPS	*Fish* and *Chips* and *Gravy*

Now complete the following:

1.

.....sharp

..........MAJOR

2.

.....sharp .....sharp

..........MAJOR

3.

.....sharp .....sharp .....sharp

..........MAJOR

SECTION 3

Second Concert Performance

Choose a tune to play either as a SOLO – on your own; or as an ENSEMBLE – with others.

Musical Signs

1. What do these signs mean?

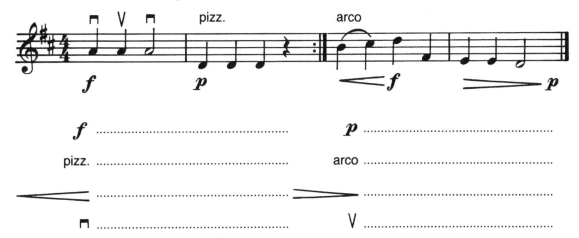

f ....   *p* ....

pizz. ....   arco ....

< ....   > ....

⊓ ....   V ....

2. Fill in the meaning of the numbered signs:

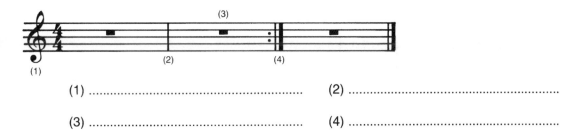

(1) ....   (2) ....

(3) ....   (4) ....

3. Add signs to this tune to make it more exciting!

The G String Notes

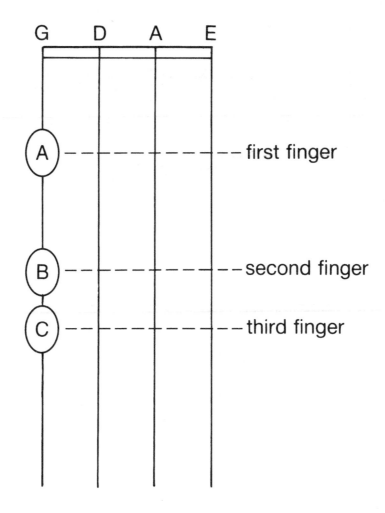

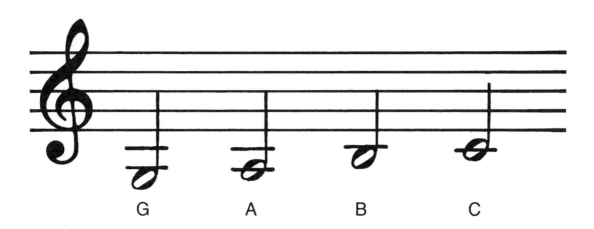

Exercises on the G String

The Scale of G Major

Now you are ready to learn the G major scale and arpeggio on page 59.

andante – at a walking pace
allegro – quick and lively

> accent
⌒ pause

Can you tap the Clog Dance rhythm with your feet? Try dancing as you play!

MAKING UP YOUR OWN TUNE

Now you are ready to start your tune. Try out these ideas:

1. Use the rhythms which you have played to make a tune on the open strings.

2. Choose one string and invent a tune using the notes on the string you have chosen.

3. Try inventing a tune using notes on any string you like.

4. Can you remember your tunes and play them again?

ECHO GAME

Ask your teacher or a friend to play these tunes to you. Try to play the same tune *WITHOUT LOOKING AT THE MUSIC*.

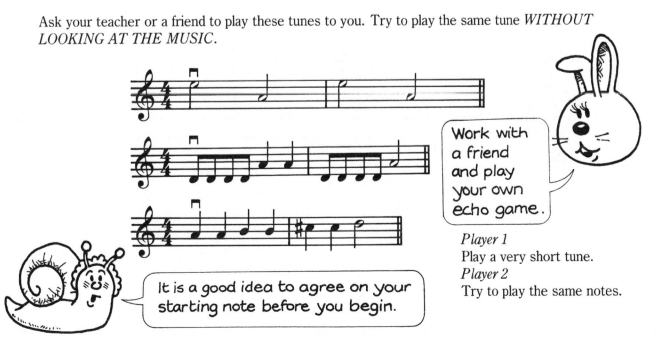

Work with a friend and play your own echo game.

Player 1
Play a very short tune.
Player 2
Try to play the same notes.

It is a good idea to agree on your starting note before you begin.

The E String Notes

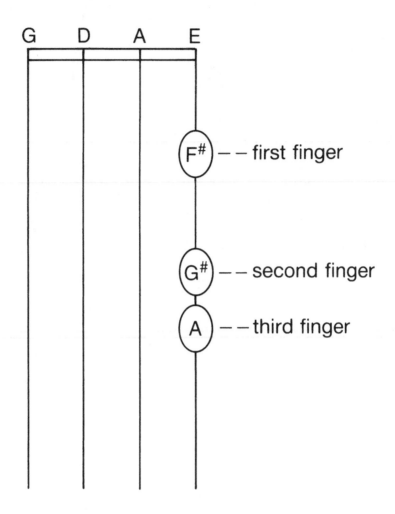

G   D   A   E

F# – – first finger

G# – – second finger

A – – third finger

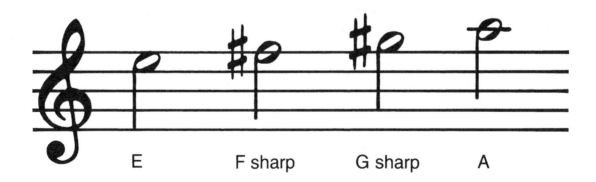

E   F sharp   G sharp   A

Exercises on the E String

Now you are ready to learn the A major scale and arpeggio on page 59.

Name the Notes (ii)

1. Notes on the D string:

....

2. Notes on the A string:

....

3. Notes on the E string:

....

4. Notes on the G string:

....

Rounds

Swans on the River

Castles in the Air

Pigs in Puddles

The Fourth Finger on the E String

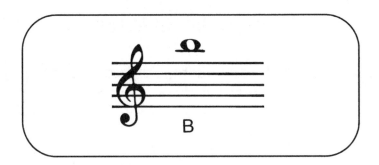

B

Leave a finger space between your third and fourth fingers.

B

The Fourth Finger Exercises

P*

1

Count: 1　2　3　4

P

2

Keep all your fingers curved on the string.

Little Bird

Little Bird – Ensemble Part

Moon Waltz

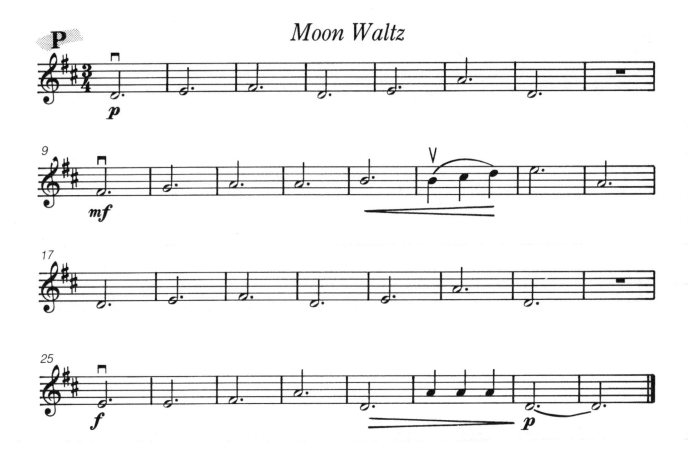

The tie

When a curved line connects two notes that are the same, it is called a tie. Both notes are played in the same bow stroke and counted as one note.

Three notes in one bow
In bar 14 three notes are connected with a slur.
Play all three notes with one up bow stroke.

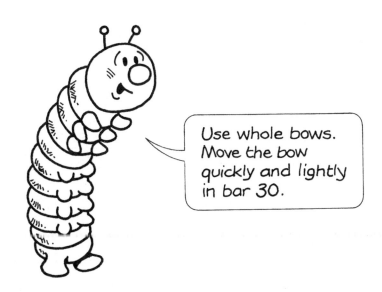

Use whole bows.
Move the bow quickly and lightly in bar 30.

Word Search

```
P  N  I  L  O  I  V  X  R  A  B  P
C  I  F  E  L  C  E  L  B  E  R  T
O  P  Z  L  R  H  Y  T  H  M  T  Y
U  R  L  Z  V  M  O  P  T  S  V  Q
N  O  M  G  I  D  C  O  E  S  Q  F
T  J  K  N  O  C  R  R  H  G  J  L
Z  A  I  I  L  P  A  N  C  H  Q  A
E  M  I  R  A  E  N  T  T  M  U  T
V  I  J  T  K  G  S  B  O  W  A  O
A  N  O  S  E  M  I  B  R  E  V  E
T  O  F  E  O  L  L  E  C  U  E  Q
S  R  U  L  S  O  I  S  H  A  R  P
```

Arco	*Flat*	*Quaver*	*Stave*
Bar	*Major*	*Rest*	*String*
Bow	*Minim*	*Rhythm*	*Treble Clef*
Cello	*Minor*	*Semibreve*	*Viola*
Count	*Peg*	*Sharp*	*Violin*
Crotchet	*Pizzicato*	*Slur*	

Third Concert Performance

Make up a concert programme from the music you have learned so far. You may play:

a solo;
or an ensemble with other violinists;
or an ensemble with violinists, viola players, or cellists.

Exercises to Help You Play in Tune!

1 Count: 1 2 3 4

2 Count: 1 2 3 4

3 Count: 1 2 3 4

4 Count: 1 2 3 4

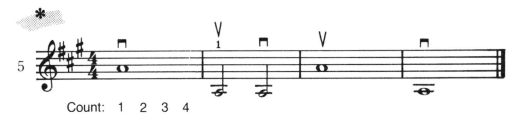

5 Count: 1 2 3 4

LISTEN !!!
Are your fingers in
the right place?

Time Signatures

This rhythm is in $\frac{4}{4}$ time. It has four crotchet beats in each bar. Clap the rhythm and count the beats:

Count: 1   2   3 + 4   1   2 + 3   4   1   2   3   4 +   1   2   3   4

This rhythm is in $\frac{3}{4}$ time. It has three crotchet beats in each bar. Clap the rhythm and count the beats:

Count: 1   2   3   1   2 + 3 +   1   2   3   1   2   3

This rhythm is in $\frac{2}{4}$ time. It has two crotchet beats in each bar. Clap the rhythm and count the beats:

Count: 1   2   1   2 +   1   2   1   2

Now write your own rhythms in the following time signatures using the note A:

1.

2.

3.

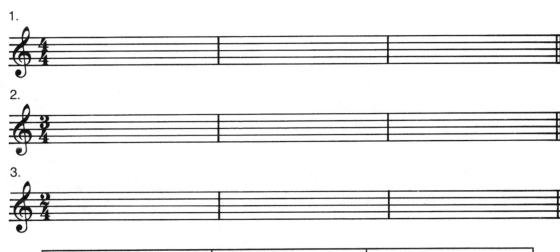

SIGHT-READING

Open string and first finger notes:

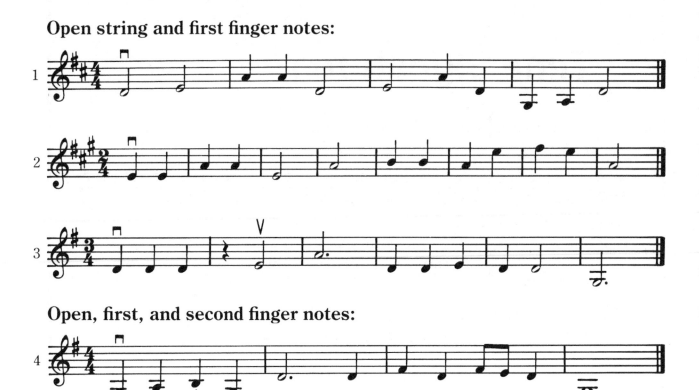

Open, first, and second finger notes:

First, second, and third finger notes:

SCALES AND ARPEGGIOS

Finger Patterns for the Scales

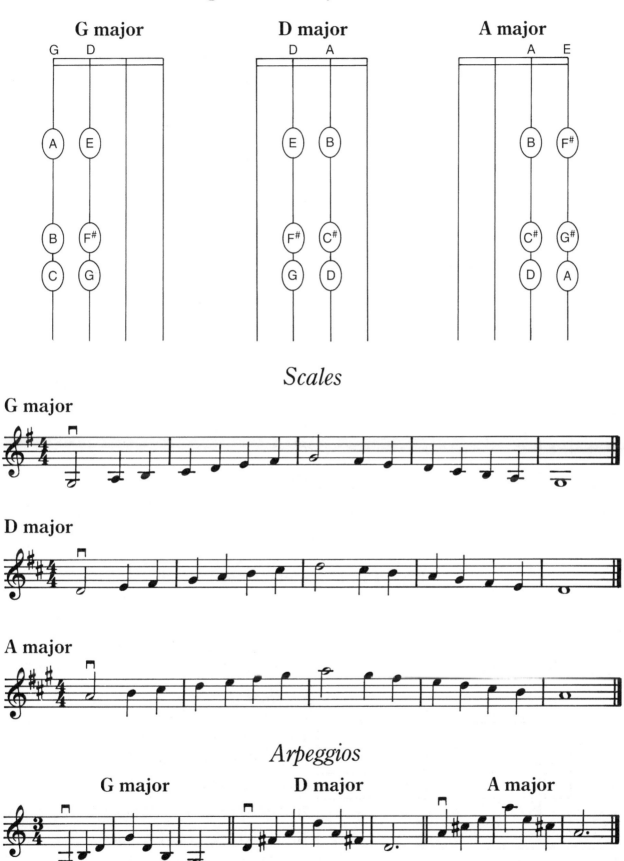

G major

D major

A major

Scales

G major

D major

A major

Arpeggios

G major

D major

A major

Try playing the scales using the rhythms on page 19.

ACHIEVEMENT RECORD

Section 1

Page	√	Comment	
6			Parts of Violin and Bow. Music Facts.
7			Care of the Instrument. Posture.
9			The Violin Strings
10			Open Strings Pizzicato
12			The Left Hand Finger Numbers
13			'Hopscotch'
13			'Hill Climbing'
13			'Moonlight'
13			'Rainbows'
13			'Jumping Jack'
13			'Fourth Finger March'
16			Note Learning Game
17			Leger Lines
18			Time Signatures. Bars and Barlines. Bowing Signs.
19			Bowing Patterns
21			The Open Strings
22			The Crotchet
23			The Minim
24			The Semibreve. Bowing Exercises on Open Strings.
25			Rests

First Concert Performance

solo . . . .   ensemble . . . .

date . . . .   music played . . . .

Section 2

Page	√	Comment	
28			The First Finger on the D String
29			The First Finger on the A String
30			Colour and Play
32			The Second Finger on the D String
33			The Second Finger on the A String
34			The Third Finger on the D String
35			The Third Finger on the A String

Page	√	Comment	
37			The Quaver. The Dotted Minim.
39			The Slur

Second Concert Performance

solo . . . . ensemble . . . .

date . . . . music played . . . .

Section 3

Page	√	Comment	
41			'Twinkle, Twinkle'
41			'Frère Jacques'
42			'Morris Tune'
42			'London Bridge'
42			'French Folk Song'
44			The G String Notes
45			Exercises on the G String
46			'Waltz in G'
46			'Clog Dance'
47			Making Up Your Own Tune
47			Echo Game
48			The E String Notes
49			Exercises on the E String
51			'Swans on the River'
51			'Castles in the Air'
51			'Pigs in Puddles'
52			The Fourth Finger on the E String
53			'Little Bird'
54			'Moon Waltz'
55			Word Search
56			Exercises to Help You Play in Tune!
58			Sight-reading
59			G Major Scale and Arpeggio
59			D Major Scale and Arpeggio
59			A Major Scale and Arpeggio

Third Concert Performance

solo . . . . ensemble . . . .

date . . . . music played . . . .

Comments on Posture and Style

	SECTION 1	SECTION 2	SECTION 3
LEFT HAND			
BOWING			
POSTURE			

Theory Worksheets

	√	COMMENT
WORKSHEET 1 – THE VIOLIN		
WORKSHEET 2 – THE BOW		
WORKSHEET 3 – BASIC KNOWLEDGE		
WORKSHEET 4 – NAME THE NOTES (i)		
WORKSHEET 5 – NOTE VALUES		
WORKSHEET 6 – KEY SIGNATURES		
WORKSHEET 7 – MUSICAL SIGNS		
WORKSHEET 8 – NAME THE NOTES (ii)		
WORKSHEET 9 – TIME SIGNATURES		

Overall Assessment

POSTURE AND STYLE	
SCALES	
ARPEGGIOS	
EXERCISES	
PIECES	
SIGHT-READING	
AURAL	
THEORY	
GENERAL COMMENT	

AUDIO TRACK NOTES

Section 3

*Tracks 12, 24–8, and 70 are for cello and piano only; tracks 13 and 68 are for violin, viola, and piano only; track 61 is for violin and piano only; track 62 is for viola, cello, and piano only.

Audio credits

Violin and viola: Jane Griffiths
Cello: Barnabas Morse-Brown
Piano: Emily Chelu

Recorded and mixed by Jon Fletcher at The Ark-T Studio, Oxford
Mastered by Tim Turan at Turan Audio, Oxford